Christmas Stories

Arnie Lightning

Arnie Lightning Books

Copyright © 2016 by Hey Sup Bye Publishing

All rights reserved. This book is a work of fiction. Graphics used in this book are licensed and © Dollar Photo Club. No part of this book or this book as a whole may be used, reproduced, or transmitted in any form or means without written permission from the publisher.

ISBN-13: 978-1535419536
ISBN-10: 1535419539

"Maybe Christmas, he thought, doesn't come from a store. Maybe Christmas, perhaps, means a little bit more."

-The Grinch

CONTENTS

FREE GIFT 1

The North Pole Penguin 3

Sophia Claus 6

Teddy the Christmas Bear 9

Bobby's Christmas Wish 12

Mistletoe Makes the Team 16

Christmas Jokes 19

Find the Differences #1 27

Find the Differences #2 28

Solutions 29

ABOUT THE AUTHOR 31

FREE GIFT

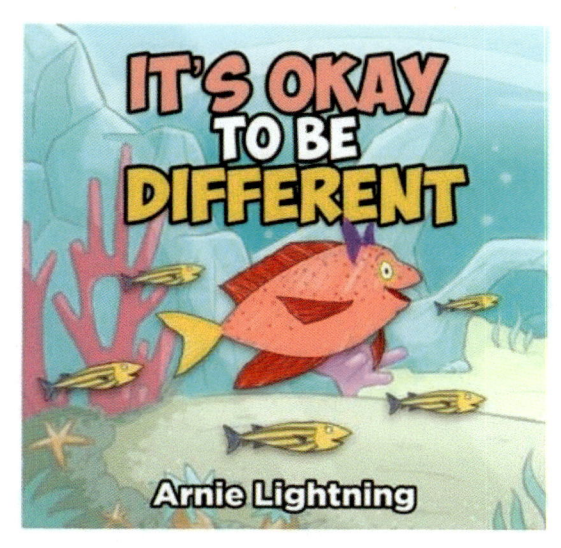

"It's Okay to Be Different" is a beautifully illustrated story about accepting and celebrating others for their differences. It's a great way to teach children to appreciate and accept others for who they are.

To claim your FREE GIFT, simply go to www.ArnieLightning.com/freegift and enter your email address. Shortly thereafter, I will send you a free eBook for you to enjoy!

Please visit: www.ArnieLightning.com/freegift

The North Pole Penguin

Polly Penguin lived in a penguin colony in the South Pole. But, unlike the other penguins, she was not happy with her home. She often wondered why she was unlucky enough to live at the South Pole. The South Pole was nothing but snow and ice.

However, Polly had heard very different things about the North Pole. According to the storybooks Mama Penguin had read to her when she was very young, the North Pole was a wonderful, magical place, the home of a kind old man named Santa Claus. Santa Claus and his elves worked hard all year, making toys for children. Then, on

Christmas Eve, they would deliver these presents by sleigh to children all around the world!

The pictures in Mama Penguin's storybooks showed the North Pole as a beautiful place full of color and good cheer, where workshops and reindeer stables stood in the snow, painted with candy-cane stripes and decorated with shimmering Christmas lights.

Santa and his wife dressed in jolly outfits of red, and the elves had jingling bells on the points of their shoes. The magical reindeer had holly and mistletoe woven into their harnesses, and the whole night shone with magic when Santa and his sleigh rose into the sky each Christmas Eve.

Compared to the North Pole, the South Pole was nothing but a big, drab slab of white and gray that seemed to stretch on forever. There was no color anywhere to be seen. Why, even Polly and the other penguins had feathers of boring black and white!

"It's not fair," thought Polly. As she grew up, she wished many times that she could live at the North Pole. So what if there weren't any other penguins there?

One year around Christmas, Polly got a wonderful idea. While all the other penguins in the colony wrote their wish-lists to Santa Claus, Penny wrote one special wish of her own. Letting go of the paper, she watched as the north wind carried it toward Santa on the other side of the world. Now, all Polly had to do was wait.

As excited as she was on Christmas Eve, Polly found that, for some strange reason, she was very tired. So, as much as she wanted to stay awake for Santa's arrival, she simply couldn't. She drifted off into a deep sleep, not waking even when Santa entered her igloo during the night.

The next thing Polly knew, it was Christmas morning. She opened her eyes and looked around. She wasn't in her igloo anymore! Instead, she was inside her own tiny house, painted with candy-stripes and sitting in the snow beside a matching reindeer stables. As Polly wandered out of the little house, she couldn't believe her eyes. There, right in front of her, was Santa's workshop itself!

Santa had granted Polly's Christmas wish and taken her to the North Pole to live. Polly danced around in the snow, enjoying the Christmassy sights and sounds and colors all around her.

How wonderful it was to be the very first penguin at the North Pole!

Christmas Activity

What do you want for Christmas? It's time to get a pencil and a piece of paper and write a letter to Santa Claus! After you write your letter be sure to send it to the address below.

Santa Claus
1 Reindeer Lane
North Pole 55055

Sophia Claus

Of course, you know all about Santa and Mrs. Claus and the elves and the reindeer. But have you ever heard of the Clauses' granddaughter, Sophia? Little Sophia Claus, you see, just might be the North Pole's best-kept secret. But without her, it would be nearly impossible for Santa to be ready on time for his annual Christmas Eve adventure.

That's because Sophia is the one who makes sure the elves stay on task. Sophia is the one who breaks up disagreements between the elves. Sophia is the one who delivers Mrs. Claus's fresh-baked goodies to Santa as he sits in his office, separating children's Christmas lists into Naughty and Nice piles. Sophia is the one who feeds the reindeer, cleans their stalls, takes care of them when they're sick, and even takes them for practice flights to get ready for the big night.

Now you see how important Sophia is! But that's not the end of it, because, one year it particular, it was up to Sophia Claus to save Christmas!

The day before Christmas Eve, both Santa and Mrs. Claus became very sick with the flu! When they woke up the next morning, neither of them was feeling any better, and Santa knew he was in no shape to take the sleigh out that night.

"What am I going to do?" he moaned to his wife. "Children all over the world are counting on me. I can't disappoint them, but I'm too sick to get out of bed!"

"I wish I could help you, dear," Mrs. Claus said, blowing her nose. "But unfortunately, I'm just as sick as you are. It looks like Christmas might have to be cancelled this year."

"Cancel Christmas?" a voice exclaimed.

The Clauses looked up to see Sophia, who was bringing them soup and hot tea.

"Yes, dear," Santa told his granddaughter. "Both your grandmother and I are too sick to deliver presents tonight."

"What about me?" Sophia asked. "I'm not sick. I know how to fly the reindeer. I've even gone with you when you make your deliveries, Grandfather. There's no reason I can't take your place this year."

The Clauses looked at each other in disbelief. Sophia was so young, and so small! Could she really handle such a big job?

"Please," Sophia begged. "Just have a little faith in me. I can do it, I promise. I'll even take the head elf with me, if that makes you feel better."

Santa looked at Mrs. Claus. Mrs. Claus sighed. They both knew that Sophia was very responsible, and they couldn't bear to disappoint the children of the world.

"All right," Santa agreed at last. "But please remember to stop for rest when you get tired, and to eat plenty of cookies and milk to keep up your strength."

"I promise!" Sophia exclaimed, overjoyed.

And what do you know? That was the one and one Christmas Eve in history when the presents were delivered by none other than Santa Claus's very own granddaughter. Sophia Claus had saved Christmas for the children of the world!

Teddy the Christmas Bear

Teddy was an old stuffed bear who lived at Santa's workshop. Although he had been made by Santa's elves many years before, Teddy was one of those few unlucky toys that have never managed to find a good home. It seemed that the elves made one too many teddy bears that year, and ever after, no one had a need for Teddy.

Each year, as Christmas rolled around again, Teddy hoped against hope that perhaps this would be the year when one special child somewhere in the world would write to Santa, asking for a teddy bear just like him, with soft brown fur and bright shoe-button eyes and a shiny plaid bow tied around his neck. But, as Christmas after

Christmas went by, and Teddy still hadn't found a home, he grew very discouraged.

"Maybe I ought to give up," thought Teddy. "I really don't think anyone is ever going to want me, at this rate."

That seemed especially true as the kids of the world became more and more fascinated with fancy electronic gadgets and computerized toys. To them, a bear like Teddy was much too simple. He couldn't walk or talk or respond to a child. He couldn't do much, in fact, except be hugged and loved and cherished.

But today's kids didn't seem too interested in that sort of thing. Teddy slumped tiredly on his shelf at the back of the workshop, watching Santa's elves finish up a batch of robotic puppies with flashing light-up eyes. They looked kind of creepy to Teddy, and he wondered why any child would prefer a hard metal robot puppy to a soft stuffed bear who could be squeezed and cuddled with.

Teddy had all but given up hope by Christmas Eve. As it grew dark over the North Pole, Santa's elves finished loading the sleigh with goodies and hitching up the reindeer.

"We're ready to roll, Santa!" Teddy heard Jingle, the head elf, call.

Santa emerged from his office, dressed in his red suit and hat. But he looked very concerned.

"Why, Chief, what's the matter?" asked Jingle.

Santa waved a piece of paper over his head. "It's this!" he said. "Poor little Karen's letter got stuck in the bottom of the mail basket, and I didn't have a chance to read it till just now! It seems that Karen is one of the few children left in the world who doesn't want some fancy toy or other for Christmas, but now there's no time left to make her what she really wants!"

"What does she want, Chief?" asked Jingle.

"A bear," replied Santa. "A simple, old-fashioned teddy bear with brown fur, shoe-button eyes, and a bow around his neck."

At the sound of that, Teddy's heart leapt. Would Jingle remember he was still here?

Teddy didn't have to wonder long.

"Chief!" cried Jingle. "You're in luck. There's a bear just like that who's been in the back for years. I'll go get him!"

So, that Christmas, both Teddy and Karen got what they wanted most of all!

Bobby's Christmas Wish

"What's on your Christmas wish-list?" asked Bobby's best friend Mark. "I asked Santa for that new pirate-ship video game, a soccer ball, and a Lego set."

Bobby lowered his voice. "If I tell you, you have to promise not to tell anybody."

Mark looked very curious. "My lips are zipped," he said.

"Okay." Bobby closed his bedroom door, just in case his pesky little sister Caroline was spying. Then he told Mark, "I asked Santa for a sleigh ride."

"What?" Mark gasped.

"I couldn't think of anything I especially wanted this year," Bobby explained. "And then I thought, what could be cooler than taking a spin in Santa's sleigh? I asked Santa to wake me up just as soon as he finishes stuffing the stockings and leaving presents for Caroline."

Mark shook his head. "I don't know," he said uncertainly. "Do you think Santa would do that?"

"I guess I'll just have to wait and see," Bobby answered.

On Christmas Eve, Bobby was so excited he could hardly sleep. He tossed and turned for hours. Then, just as he was finally dozing off, the clicking sound of reindeer hooves on the roof jolted him wide awake!

"Santa's here!" Bobby thought, shivering with anticipation. He lay still, barely breathing, and listened as Santa climbed out of his sleigh and laughed a jolly, "Ho, ho, ho!"

Then Santa slipped down Bobby's chimney. Bobby could hear him landing in the living-room. "This is too cool!" thought Bobby, who had never been awake for Santa's arrival before.

Minutes ticked by. Bobby imagined that Santa was filling the Christmas stockings and leaving Caroline's presents under the tree. After that, Bobby figured, he was probably resting a moment to enjoy the cookies and milk that were waiting for him.

At longest last, Bobby heard the sound he had been waiting for. Santa was climbing the stairs to his room! Did that mean Santa was actually going to grant Bobby's wish and take him for a sleigh ride?

Bobby squeezed his eyes shut, pretending to be sleeping.

A moment later, his bedroom door creaked open, and a kind voice said, "Wake up, Bobby! Merry Christmas!"

Trembling with excitement, Bobby opened his eyes to see none other than Santa Claus himself! "M-merry Christmas, Santa," he stammered.

"Are you ready to join me in my sleigh?" Santa asked, his blue eyes twinkling.

"Am I ever!" Bobby couldn't wait to tell Mark that his Christmas wish had come true! He put on his coat and boots and shinnied up the chimney with Santa.

There, on the roof, stood Santa's sleigh, led by a team of eight reindeer. It was shiny and red, loaded down with presents for the children of the world. Bobby was still having a hard time believing his eyes when Santa lifted him into the sleigh for the Christmas Eve ride of his life!

"On Dasher, on Dancer!" Santa began, slapping the reins across the reindeer's backs.

And before Bobby knew it, he was soaring through the sky in Santa's sleigh, just as he had wished!

Mistletoe Makes the Team

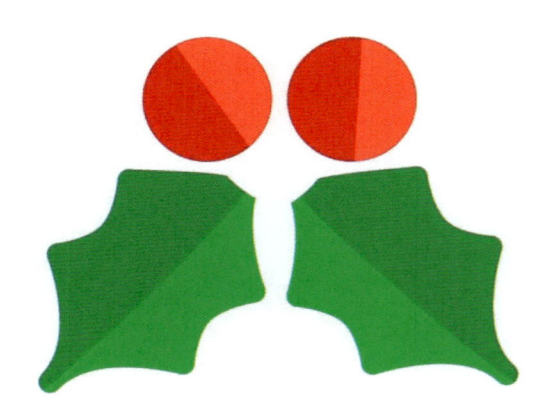

"Sleigh Team Tryouts Tonight," read the snow-caked sign at the entrance to the reindeer stables. Underneath, in smaller letters, it said, "Calling all strong young bucks!"

Mistletoe the reindeer sighed. It just wasn't fair that only boy reindeer were allowed to try out for the sleigh team. Ever since the day she was born, Mistletoe had wanted nothing more than to pull Santa's sleigh through the starry dark night on Christmas Eve, delivering gifts to children all around the world.

But it looked like her dream would never come true. For some reason, Santa seemed to prefer boy reindeer to pull his sleigh. Mistletoe knew she was swift and strong and could do a wonderful job—but how could she prove that to Santa if she wasn't invited to try out for the sleigh team?

That night, the entire North Pole was full of Christmas cheer. Santa and Mrs. Claus, the elves, the reindeer, and everyone else who called the North Pole "home" had gathered to enjoy Christmas cookies and cocoa as they watched the tryouts. It was a crisp, snowy night, and the Christmas lights on the trees and stables and Santa's workshop shimmered and shone.

Some of Mistletoe's reindeer friends were singing Christmas carols and cheering for the bucks who were trying out, but Mistletoe's heart wasn't in it. She watched as buck after buck soared clear across the sky before landing in the snow next to Santa. Some of them were better fliers than others. Most of them were pretty good. But Mistletoe ached inside. If only Santa would let her try out!

All of a sudden, something across the clearing caught Mistletoe's attention. A baby polar bear had gotten tangled in the holly bushes and was crying for help! Mistletoe looked around to see if anyone else had noticed, but they were all too distracted. Mistletoe knew she had to help!

Without thinking twice, she leapt gracefully into the air with all the strength and speed of Santa's best reindeer. She slowed when she reached the other side of the clearing and made a clean landing right beside the holly bushes. Not realizing that everyone at the sleigh team tryouts had stopped to watch her, Mistletoe used her mouth to pull branches aside until the polar bear cub was free.

"Thank you," whimpered the grateful little bear, and Mistletoe smiled and offered to walk him home to his mommy.

When she returned to the clearing, Mistletoe was surprised to hear Santa say, "There you are! We've been waiting for you, Mistletoe!"

"You have?" asked Mistletoe.

"Absolutely," replied Santa. "We all saw you fly across the clearing to rescue that baby bear. Mistletoe, I had no idea you were such a strong flier. Why, you're just what my team needs! That is, if you'll accept the job?"

Mistletoe could hardly keep the joy out of her voice as she said, "Santa, I'd be honored!"

And from that day on, Santa has opened the sleigh team tryouts for boy and girl reindeer alike!

Christmas Jokes

Q: Why does Santa go down the chimney?

A: Because it soots him!

Q: What do snowmen like most about going to school?

A: Snow and tell!

Q: What's Santa called when he takes a rest while delivering presents?

A: Santa Pause!

Q: When is a good time for Santa to visit?

A: Anytime!

Q: What songs do Santa's elves sing to him when he comes home freezing on Christmas night?

A: Freeze a jolly good fellow!

Q: Why couldn't the skeleton go to the Christmas Party?

A: He had no body to go with!

Q: How did the chickens dance at the Christmas party?

A: Chick to chick!

Q: Who delivers presents to baby sharks at Christmas?

A: Santa Jaws!

Q: Why is a cat on a beach like Christmas?

A: Because they both have sandy claws!

Q: Why did Rudolph wear sunglasses at the beach?

A: He didn't want to be recognized!

Q: What do snowmen eat for breakfast?

A: Snowflakes!

Q: What did they call Santa after he lost his pants?

A: Saint Knickerless!

Q: What nationality is Santa Claus?

A: North Polish!

Q: What can Santa give away and still keep?

A: A cold!

Q: How do sheep in Mexico say Merry Christmas?

A: Fleece Navidad!

Q: Where does Frosty the Snowman keep his money?

A: In the snowbank!

Q: Why is it so cold at Christmas?

A: Because it's in Decembrrr!

Q: What is Tarzan's favorite Christmas song?

A: Jungle bells!

Q: How does Santa Claus take pictures?

A: With his North Pole-aroid!

Q: What did Mrs. Claus say to Santa as they were looking out the window?

A: Looks like rain dear (reindeer)!

Q: Which reindeer has the worst manners?

A: Rude-olph!

Q: What does Santa call that reindeer with no eyes?

A: No-eyed-deer!

Q: What was the hairdresser's favorite Christmas song?

A: Oh Comb All Ye Faithful!

Q: Who delivers cat Christmas presents?

A: Santa Claws!

Q: What is red then white and red then white?

A: Santa rolling down a snowy hill!

Q: What's Scrooge's favorite Christmas game?

A: Mean-opoly!

Find the Differences #1

FIND 10 DIFFERENCES

Find the Differences #2

FIND
10
DIFFERENCES

Solutions

FIND **10** DIFFERENCES

FIND 10 DIFFERENCES

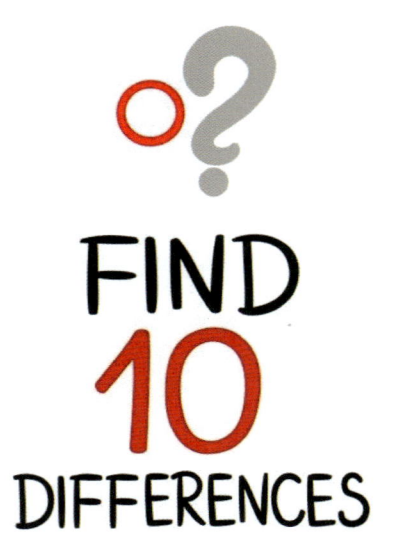

ABOUT THE AUTHOR

Arnie Lightning is a dreamer. He believes that everyone should dream big and not be afraid to take chances to make their dreams come true. Arnie enjoys writing, reading, doodling, and traveling. In his free time, he likes to play video games and run. Arnie lives in Mississippi where he graduated from The University of Southern Mississippi in Hattiesburg, MS.

For more books by Arnie Lightning please visit:
www.ArnieLightning.com/books

Printed in Great Britain
by Amazon